# DISCOVERING JESUS

## A 21-DAY DEVOTIONAL THROUGH THE GOSPEL OF JOHN

### RUBEN A. RAMOS

WESTBOW
PRESS®
A DIVISION OF THOMAS NELSON
& ZONDERVAN

WestBow Press books may be ordered through booksellers or by contacting:

WestBow Press
A Division of Thomas Nelson & Zondervan
1663 Liberty Drive
Bloomington, IN 47403
www.westbowpress.com
844-714-3454

Scripture quotations marked NIV are taken from The Holy Bible, New International Version®, NIV® Copyright © 1973, 1978, 1984, 2011 by Biblica, Inc.® Used by permission. All rights reserved worldwide.

Scripture quotations marked NKJV are taken from the New King James Version®. Copyright © 1982 by Thomas Nelson. Used by permission. All rights reserved.

ISBN: 978-1-6642-5053-6 (sc)
ISBN: 978-1-6642-5054-3 (e)

Library of Congress Control Number: 2021923547

Print information available on the last page.

WestBow Press rev. date: 02/08/2022

# PREFACE

"Well, what does that mean?"

That's a question I get asked a lot. People coming to the faith for the first time who are curious to know what this whole Christian faith is like ask a lot of questions most of which just need basic answers, but often, Christians give them long-winded explanations that leave them just more confused. We tell them that the scripture they are looking at reflects Isaiah's writings in chapter 53 and how that points to the Messiah in Revelation after the dragon comes. "Wait. Dragon? What's going on here?" Well-meaning people give new believers answers to questions they didn't ask.

I have noticed that well-intended people speak to those who are new to the faith as if everyone in the room has the same knowledge, understanding of biblical culture, and even the same worldview. I'm sure it can be frustrating for people to hear someone speak about Jesus, a person they're genuinely interested in, but not understand what is being said, but we do this often and sometimes unintentionally.

A big desire I have is to bring clarity to people who don't understand Christianity. I don't want to present the Bible to others with a thousand assumptions in our conversations. I want them to know that I want to meet them where they are because I think that's what Jesus would do.

In the next twenty-one days, we'll read through the book of John. You might be thinking, *Why that book of the Bible?* Well, the gospel of John is one of the easiest to understand. Additionally, studies suggest that it takes around twenty-one days to develop a habit. The gospel of John is twenty-one chapters long. So if we want to create a habit of reading Scripture, this works out great for us!

To give some context, John was a disciple, or a student, of Jesus; he was one of the original twelve disciples and one of Jesus's closest friends. You'll see as you read John that there are a few times when Jesus took a smaller group with Him; that group included Peter, James, and John. John even nicknamed himself "the one Jesus loved." I guess if you're the one writing the book, you can give yourself whatever nickname you want.

As we walk through this together, I want you to read the chapter that corresponds with the day; on day 1, read John 1 and so on. When you read through each section of this book, you'll notice that a portion is highlighted and talked about, but that's not meant to say it's the only thing worth taking out of the text. You'll find things in that chapter that stand out to you, and that's a good thing! I'm highlighting this portion of the text to share with you something important in understanding Jesus's nature.

You'll also see a Discovery statement. This will help you identify the key idea we discuss and will give you a single thought to hold onto for the rest of the day.

You don't have to have it all together or know everything about the Bible to get to know this God it talks about. It's not about knowing the perfect religious formula; it's about discovering a relationship with Jesus for yourself.

# VISIBLE
## JOHN 1

**H**ave you ever looked through your parents' photo albums? Not just one when you were little; I mean those from before you were born. Maybe your mom wore pants that you can't believe. I remember seeing an old picture of my dad in a mesh shirt that would surely get him arrested today.

It's wild to think that our parents had lives before we came into the picture. They had childhoods, fun experiences, and heartbreaks. At one time, the thought of us hadn't even crossed their minds!

In the opening words of the gospel of John, this follower of Jesus explained who He was before anything else. John explained that Jesus was there even at the beginning—not just before His mom and dad. He was there before their moms and dads, before *their* moms and dads, and before *their* moms and dads. You get my point.

The Bible opens with God creating the world, and John wrote about how Jesus existed with God back then. We know Jesus was there because John wrote that the Word (Jesus) gave life to everything that was created and that in the life, there was light. And that light shines in the darkness so strongly that it completely extinguished the darkness.

This is the Jesus we'll be looking at. God can be difficult for us to wrap our minds around, but Jesus is a concept we can better understand. This is the God that existed way before anything else and the God we can see and know today. Jesus is the God we can see, the God who knows what it's like to be human including how to feel joy, sorrow, love, and pain. While God can seem abstract, Jesus was sent for us to visibly see. He's not just a faraway being we have no connection with. He's not like old photos that have little to do with our lives now. He is the God who came near to know what you and I deal with. Not only that, but in Him, the darkness of death, sin, and even our current difficulties don't stand a chance.

**Discovery**
Jesus is the God we can see.

# DYED
## JOHN 2

With dyed fabric, you can see the results of a process that took days to get to the right color. And when the color seeped into the fabric, it went so deep that it couldn't be removed.

In John 2, Jesus was at a wedding in Cana. When all the wine was gone, Mary, Jesus's mother, told the servants to let Jesus know and do whatever He said. Jesus turned barrels of what was once water into wine that was so delicious that the master of ceremonies couldn't believe the best wine had been saved for last. The wine the master of ceremonies tasted was once water, but he remarked how everything about it was changed.

When we have a true life-changing experience with Jesus, He'll change our lives so dramatically that people won't recognize us. Yes, we'll still be the same us, but how we look and act will begin to be different from how we once looked and acted.

We might have frequently talked about others in a negative light, tried to make a coworker look bad in front of a boss, or torn people down with our words. But after we recognize who Jesus is, our lives look completely different.

Just like dyed fabric, what Jesus does for us completely changes who we are. When we experience Jesus, we can't go back to who we used to be. He completely washes away our sins, and we are different. We were once one thing, but our encounter with Jesus has made us new.

**Discovery**
Jesus dramatically changes our lives.

# QUESTIONS
## JOHN 3

**M**any people are scared to ask questions about faith. They get to this place where they feel that having faith in Jesus means that they have to have all the answers or give up asking questions. I've been serving Jesus for more than ten years and have been in ministry for seven, but eve I don't have all the answers.

In John 3, we see Nicodemus, a religious leader, at night. He was nervous. He didn't feel that he should be asking Jesus questions. Because he had been serving God for so long, he thought that he should know for sure whether this Jesus was the promised Messiah who was going to take away the sins of the world. But there he was approaching Jesus at night with lots of questions.

What I find the most comforting in this chapter is that Jesus didn't ignore Nicodemus; He didn't dismiss Nicodemus as a terrible person for asking questions. Instead, He explained to Nicodemus exactly what He had come to do, and the most important thing that Jesus explained was why He was here to do it. This is one of the most famous verses in the New Testament; it's one of the top-ranked searches of the Bible, it's tattooed on people's bodies, and it's even been written on the faces of football players: "For God so loved the world that he gave his one and only Son, that whoever believes in him shall not perish but have eternal life" (John 3:16 NIV).

Jesus didn't ridicule Nicodemus for having questions about who He was. Instead, Jesus explained that even in his questions, He still loved Nicodemus.

**Discovery**
Even in your questions, Jesus still loves you.

# SOURCE
## JOHN 4

**W**e all need certain things to provide for our families. Some people need a car to travel, a chainsaw to cut down trees, or maybe a certain skill or tool to do what they need to get the job done. We may need a laptop to prepare presentations, write emails, or order products.

In John 4, Jesus met a woman at a well. After He told her that He was the living water and proved it by telling her all her deepest secrets, she dropped the most important thing she had— her bucket. She used it every day to fetch water, a very basic need. This was an essential tool to provide for herself and her family. But she left her bucket behind, headed into town, and told everyone who Jesus was. She gave up her main source to provide for herself for a true Source that would better provide for her.

Now, Jesus wasn't advocating that she should never drink water again. Please drink water. It's good for your skin. But rather, He was showing her that He was the true Source that sustains life.

It's easy for us to get into a place where we hold onto what we're used to. You might be thinking, *I've been doing this one thing this one way for years, so why would I suddenly do something differently?* We change because our Source has changed. We're no longer in the same old place with the same old source to provide for us. Now that doesn't necessarily mean that God is saying that we have to quit our jobs and go somewhere else, but it means that we have to stop holding onto our old sources and start beholding a better Source.

**Discovery**
Jesus is the better Source.

# LET GO
## JOHN 5

**H**ave you ever given the wrong answer to a question? Here's what I mean.

"Do you want to go to Chick-fil-A or Chipotle for lunch?"

"Yes I do!"

That didn't really answer the question, did it?

In this chapter, Jesus interacted with a man who needed physical healing. When Jesus asked him if he wanted to get well, he said, "How am I going to do that?" Jesus gave him a yes or no question, but the man replied with what he was capable of.

Here's why this is key to the passage: Jesus wasn't asking, "Why didn't you get there?" but rather, "Do you want to get there?" He was not expressing frustration with the man that he wasn't able to do the right thing. This man might have thought that Jesus was disappointed with him. He wasn't asking him because he wanted the man to be quicker, more cunning, or better. Jesus was asking because He wanted to do the work for the man.

Society puts this pressure on us to think that we have to have it all together or do it all by ourselves to prove we're worth something. There are times where we even think that we have to get everything right in our lives before we can approach God. We think that God expects us to be whole on our own before we can come to Him. He's not looking for that. He's looking for our desire—our faith—not our ability. The heart change that needs to happen in our lives comes from depending more on Jesus, not from our trying harder.

This isn't to negate how we participate in what Jesus does. Note that this man still had to pick up his own mat and walk. Our involvement isn't obsolete, but we're not striving to do God's part.

When Jesus asks if we want to be well, He's not asking us to try harder. He's asking us to let Him do the work.

**Discovery**
Jesus is asking us to let Him to do the work.

# BREAD
## JOHN 6

One of Jesus's most well-known miracles was when He took five loaves of bread and two fish that a young kid had and was able to feed 5,000 people with that. Well, actually, it was more than 5,000 because back when John was writing this account, they usually counted only men, not women or children. People often estimate that there were between 12,000 to 15,000 people there. That's impressive. There's some good stuff in that.

It's also interesting to look at this story and note that the young boy had offered his lunch to Jesus. It wasn't a lot, and most people would have patted him on the head and said, "Oh thanks, Timmy, but that just won't do." But that's not what Jesus did. He took what the little kid offered and made much of very little. There's some good stuff in that too.

But a very important part of John 6 is when the

people came to Jesus after He had fed them all that food. They were seeking Him because they wanted more of what He could do for them. After trying to get Jesus to continue to feed them, He said, "I am the bread of life. Whoever comes to me will never go hungry, and whoever believes in me will never be thirsty" (John 6:35 NIV). That was the first of Jesus's "I Am" statements. What He was stating was that He was the one who would sustain them. They came to Jesus because they wanted all Jesus could do for them, but God had sent Jesus so He could be with them.

What John was trying to communicate was that when we are with Jesus, we find our satisfaction in Him. Will Jesus do incredible things in our lives? Absolutely. But here, He's saying that He is the Bread of Life that sustains more than anything else can. He was explaining that we are called to seek the Giver of the gift, not the gift itself.

### Discovery
Jesus is the Bread of Life that sustains more than anything else can.

# REFLECT
## JOHN 7

**H**ave you ever realized that when you hang around certain people, you start picking up some of their habits? Maybe you weren't a coffee drinker but had a friend who was. After trying it once, you find yourself months down the road explaining to people the differences in roast levels and how coffee can have different notes of flavor based on the region it was grown.

In John 7, Jesus explained to the religious leaders, "Let anyone who is thirsty come to me and drink" (John 7:37 NIV). Do you know what Jesus said is the prerequisite for coming to Him? Being thirsty. That's it. He didn't list a long set of requirements such as a certain level of education, number of years of experience following the Bible perfectly, or wearing the right clothing. He simply said that if you were thirsty, come to Him.

How He followed up this statement also stands out. Jesus said, "Whoever believes in me, as the

Scripture said, 'from his innermost being will flow rivers of living water'" (John 7:38 NIV). If you remember from John 4, Jesus called Himself the living water. So how could it be that someone who came to Jesus was also the living water? It's because you become like those you surround yourself with. That doesn't mean you're suddenly going to start levitating and doubling everyone's lunch orders with just a flick of the wrist. (But if that happens to you, call me. I got questions.) Rather, we become a conduit of the living water (Jesus) that is in us.

As we spend more time with Jesus, as we discover more about Him and begin to really treasure who He is in our lives, our lives begin to align with His. As we understand Jesus more, people take notice. What the world will understand about Jesus will come from what they see us reflect of Him.

This passage shows us that the more we thirst for God, the more we become like Him. And the more we become like Him, the more we can show the world who He is.

### Discovery
What others will understand about Jesus will come from what they see us reflect of Him.

# LIGHT
## JOHN 8

The worst part about moving furniture is waking up in the middle of the night to use the bathroom and forgetting where you moved your furniture to. All of a sudden you stub your toe and you're sure they'll have to amputate this time. Something that was in the dark has suddenly been discovered (by your now broken toe) and has seriously hurt you.

In John 8, Jesus said, "I am the Light of the world. He who follows Me shall not walk in darkness, but have the light of life" (John 8:12 NIV). This is Jesus's second I Am statement. What's important to note here is that this I Am statement follows Jesus's interacting with a woman who was caught in adultery. The religious leaders at the time wanted to stone her to death, but Jesus stepped in and told them that those among them who had not sinned could start casting stones. One by one, they all left because all of them at some point had sinned. When they were gone, Jesus told the woman that He didn't condemn her and that she should go and sin no more.

When we follow Him, the Light of the World, He'll expose the dark, hidden parts of our lives to us. But just as He did for the woman, He will show His loving-kindness, which will lead us to repentance, to turn from sin. Jesus isn't looking to expose the sin in our lives to embarrass us; He wants to reveal to us where we might be living in darkness and how that can lead to us hurting ourselves. He isn't looking to condemn us but to give us the light of life.

William L. Watkinson says, "It is far better to light the candle than to curse the darkness". If we want to conquer the darkness in our lives—the sin that's in our lives—it's better to allow the Light of the World to shine in those areas and bring to light whatever doesn't belong to Him.

## Discovery
Jesus isn't looking to condemn you but to give you the light of life.

# STORY

## JOHN 9

**W**ho was the first to notice that you changed? Maybe your friends noticed that you weren't at the party *everyone* went to. Maybe you used to joke around with people, but it was actually hurting them. Now, you're encouraging people whenever you can. Maybe you ran into someone you know at a gas station and he caught that you had a way about yourself that you didn't have previously.

In today's chapter, we meet a blind man. When he interacted with Jesus, he was healed of his blindness. Soon after his miracle, the man was brought to the religious leaders, who couldn't believe that it was the same man; they accused him of lying about how he was healed.

As we walk through our new life change, we'll interact with plenty of people who will be upset about our decision to follow Jesus, who don't understand why our lives have shifted so much.

People might even question if it's even possible for us to change. But this is really an opportunity for us to share what has happened in our lives just as the blind man did; he shared about what Jesus had done in his life regardless of the proper training. He didn't go to a prestigious school to get a degree in Jesus. He did study under another religious leader for ten years before talking about his faith. He didn't know the perfect words to share, but he did know what happened to him: "One thing I do know. I was blind but now I see!" (John 9:25 NIV). Don't dismiss the significance of your story.

**Discovery**
Don't dismiss the significance of your story.

# TELL AND SHOW
## JOHN 10

**T**here's a good chance that the idea of shepherds can be lost on us if we live in the western hemisphere. We get an overall idea, but it might not actually connect much for us. But when Jesus was walking on the earth, it was very common. Shepherds were everywhere. Being a shepherd was a humble job, but if you were a good shepherd, it could be dangerous. Good shepherds would defend their sheep against wild animals, would guide their sheep to food and water, and would search tirelessly for their sheep if they got lost.

In today's passage, Jesus described Himself in two ways—the Good Shepherd and the Gate for the sheep, His third and fourth I Am statements.

Just like a good shepherd would act in the ancient Middle East, Jesus calls us to Him. And when we are His, we get to know His voice and respond to Him. Jesus, the Good Shepherd, is willing to fight for us to the point of laying down His life (John 10:11).

Jesus said that He is the Gate for the sheep. To best understand this, we have to know something about ancient Middle Eastern shepherding practices. Shepherds traveling long distances could stop at what would look like an animal pen to sleep. Here, they would be able to lead all their sheep into that pen and all sleep out in the field together. But these pens had no doors. The shepherd would then lie in front of the opening of the pen to act as a door. With him at the doorway, he would be able to make sure no sheep left and no predatory animals got in. His sheep were protected.

So when Jesus said He was the Gate for the sheep, He was saying that He was the one keeping us safe. That's why Jesus said, "[The sheep] will come in and go out, and find pasture. The thief comes only to steal and kill and destroy; I have come that they may have life, and have it to the full" (John 10:10 NIV).

These two concepts are meant be understood together. Jesus doesn't just say He's a Good Shepherd; He shows it. How He shows that is through being the Gate for His sheep.

**Discovery**
Jesus doesn't just say He's a good Shepherd; He shows it.

# COMPASSION
## JOHN 11

One thing I love about how John writes about Jesus is the way he constantly showed Jesus's humanity. We've touched on how truly divine Jesus is—healing the blind man, turning water into wine, and being able to know everything about a person. You may have heard it said that Jesus was fully God and fully human. In this chapter, we can see that in Him.

Here, Jesus caught word that His friend Lazarus had been sick and had died. When He got to the tomb, He explained to Lazarus's sister the He was the Resurrection and the Life. This is the fifth I Am statement. His sharing this with Martha was Jesus reminding her of His divinity—that He had power over the grave itself. Yet when Jesus saw His friends crying, being moved in spirit and troubled by Lazarus's death, Jesus wept.

Jesus was burdened by the death of His friend. He was deeply saddened. And it was not a single, pretty tear that rolled down His cheek. The original language used here was meant to describe that Jesus was seriously, emotionally hurt.

But even with the pain He felt, He was able to bring Lazarus to life. Jesus took the perfect opportunity to explain that He was the Resurrection and the Life; that He was divine. But He also took a moment to reveal that He was the God who knows us in our hurts and burdens because He has felt hurt and burdened too. We don't have to shy away from sharing our deepest hurts with Him because He can handle it. Jesus is both the powerful God and compassionate human.

## Discovery

Jesus is both the powerful God and compassionate human.

# LOSE
## JOHN 12

**H**ave you ever asked a toddler to share a toy that he really loves? You'll get a look that is a combination of confusion and anger. You might have an easier time asking him to explain quantum mechanics than getting your hands on that toy.

In today's passage, Jesus explained that anyone who loved his or her life would ultimately end up losing it, and in contrast, whoever lost his or her life would find it. Your Bible might even use the phrase "hate their lives." He was not suggesting that we abuse ourselves here nor is He suggesting that we shouldn't enjoy things in our lives like friends, families, vacations, and activities. Instead, He was purposely using extreme language to show that we can't hold in high value what the world around us holds. Our lives aren't meant to be lived to own the biggest house on the block, have the highest income, or have the most Instagram-worthy life. Our lives are meant to honor God, not this world.

Jesus said, "Whoever serves me must follow me; and where I am, my servant also will be. My Father will honor the one who serves me" (John 12:26 NIV). As we live to honor God, He sees that and honors us. That honor might look different for everyone, but the point is to use our lives to bring God glory, not to fill our lives with things for the sake of keeping up with the Joneses.

We can't hold onto materialistic things the way a toddler holds onto a beloved toy. If we lose our lives to serve and honor God, He will honor us in return.

**Discovery**
If we lose our lives to serve and honor God, He will honor us in return.

# ACTION
## JOHN 13

**H**ave you ever heard of love languages? It's an idea popularized by Gary Chapman and suggests people give and receive love through five distinct categories—giving and receiving gifts, words of affirmation, quality time, physical touch, and acts of service. These are great to know about yourself and about others around you.

Imagine that the way you give and receive love is very different from the way someone you care about gives and receives it. It would be difficult to love that person as he or she would want to be loved. It would also be an incredible selfless act to do that considering that that isn't your natural response to showing love.

In today's passage, we see Jesus eating Passover with His disciples, a meal typical of Jewish people celebrating them fleeing abuse in Egypt. Here, Jesus wrapped an apron around His waist and began to wash the disciples' feet. That threw them off. That was a job for a servant, not the Son of God. Yet Jesus was doing this work one foot at a time—placing it in a basin, cleaning every inch, and wiping it dry.

Toward the end of this chapter, Jesus said, "Love one another. As I have loved you, so you must live one another" (John 13:34 NIV). This was no accident that an act of love was shown before the command to love was presented. Jesus showed His disciples that love was action. To show love to one another, we must act out that love. It's not exclusively about washing feet, but doing something even if it makes us uncomfortable to show how Jesus has loved and served us. Whenever we serve someone, especially when it's uncomfortable for us, we show the character of Jesus, who first served us.

## Discovery
Jesus showed His disciples that love was action. Whenever we serve someone, especially when it's uncomfortable for us, we show the character of Jesus, who first served us.

# LOST
## JOHN 14

**G**etting lost is never fun. The second I'm not a hundred percent sure if I'm going the right way, I turn on the GPS on my phone to make sure I don't miss a single turn.

In Jesus's sixth I Am statement, He said, "I am the Way, and the Truth, and the Life" (John 14:6 NIV). Here's what's true about every person. At the end of the day, when we lay our heads on our pillows, what we're all looking for is forgiveness, for our lives to be more than just the seventy or eighty years we have, and longing for it to be full of deep meaning. It doesn't matter how successful we look on the outside; we all fundamentally want these things. We're all looking to be set right, wanting there to be something past this life, and wanting to know our lives meant something. The good news is that Jesus answers all three of these things. He is the Way to forgiveness. He is the

Truth to heaven. He is the solution to a fulfilling, meaningful life.

And the best part is that if for a second we begin to forget these things, Jesus says that He sends an Advocate, the Holy Spirit, to teach us and remind of everything He has said to us. It's a gift given to us.

## Discovery

Jesus is the Way to forgiveness. He is the Truth to heaven. He is the solution to a fulfilling, meaningful life.

# REST
## JOHN 15

The idea of working hard to achieve a goal permeates our culture. We work longer hours to prove to our bosses that we're worthy of raises. We lift more weight at the gym to show others that we're stronger than we look. We buy things we can't afford to impress people we don't know.

In today's passage, Jesus gave us His last I Am statement: "I am the Vine; you are the branches. If you remain in me and I in you, you will bear much fruit; apart from me you can do nothing" (John 15:5 NIV). This means for us to rest in Christ. In our culture, which constantly tells us that we have to work harder to achieve something, Jesus says that we have to rest in Him. To get closer to Christ, we are called to rest in Him, not push ourselves so hard that we create unrealistic views of what it looks like to try to get closer to God.

You might have heard it said that other

religions are about us trying to get closer to God. Christianity is about God getting close to us.

So what does it look like to abide? It really comes down to us beholding or recognizing who Christ is and what He did for us. When we can go back to the finished work of Jesus on the cross and how that was a great act for us to be brought to God, it reminds us of how amazing God's love for us is. When we begin to understand even just a little bit more what He did, we come to a place where we no longer want to live as we used to but instead how Christ calls us to live.

That might sound lazy to you. You might be thinking, *But what do I do? What are my actionable items?* And though I get the nature of that question, a pattern in the Bible is that those who truly recognize who Jesus is feel compelled to honor God with what happens in their lives not just through action, but through heart change. The key motivation of it all comes from resting in Christ.

**Discovery**
To get closer to Christ, we are called to rest in Him.

# GIFT
## JOHN 16

**H**ave you ever known people who are great gift givers? Somehow, they know your style, they know your favorite color, and they know the perfect time to give you that gift. Whenever that happens, we say, "Wow! You shouldn't have!" But we're so glad they did. Then you meet others who aren't so good at it and you say, "Wow … You shouldn't have," but that time you mean it.

In this passage, Jesus was in the middle of sharing some of the last things He wanted His disciples to know. He was talking about His upcoming death and was letting His followers understand the last things they'd need to know before He died.

One of those things He shared about was the Holy Spirit. Jesus said, "When He, the Spirit of truth, comes He will guide you into all truth" (John 16:13 NIV). If you remember from our reading of John 14, Jesus also said, "But the Advocate, the

Holy Spirit, whom the Father will send in my name, will teach you all things and will remind you of everything I have said to you" (John 14:26 NIV). The Holy Spirit is a gift from God to us to guide us and remind us of all truth. He dwells in us (John 14:16) helping us live lives that bring glory to God.

You may be asking, "How do I know the Holy Spirit is in me?" If you've accepted Jesus as Lord, the Holy Spirit dwells in you. It's as simple as that.

The conversation about the Holy Spirit may seem strange at first, but it's not meant to be. Remember that when Jesus promised to give the Holy Spirit, He followed that by saying that He was giving us peace (John 14:27, 16:33). The Holy Spirit isn't weird. He is a gift from God to guide us and empower us.

**Discovery**
The Holy Spirit is a gift from God to guide us and empower us.

# UNITY
## JOHN 17

In today's passage, Jesus was in the middle of a prayer. What's interesting to note here is though this whole section is a prayer of Jesus, He spent the least amount of time praying for Himself and a significant amount of time praying for others.

Jesus took time to pray for His disciples, the twelve who were with Him throughout His earthly journey. He prayed that the evil one, Satan, wouldn't harm them. Then He prayed for all believers. John recorded a time when Jesus prayed for you and me. And out of all the things He could have prayed for, He prayed that we believers would be unified. He didn't pray that everyone would have perfect theology. He didn't pray that we all had mansions. He didn't pray for each of us to be snapped out of existence the second we accepted the message of Christ. He prayed that each of us would be unified with each other.

The unity Jesus talked about isn't about

all of us holding hands and singing around a campfire. That unity is meant "so that the world may believe that [God] has sent [Jesus]" (John 17:21 NIV). Jesus calls us to be unified with other believers regardless of race, ethnicity, gender, or denomination so that those outside of the faith will know that Jesus is who He said He is.

As we walk out this faith journey, we'll interact with people who will irk us or straight up offend us, but we don't have to live in that offense. A follower of Jesus who suffered a lot of persecution for his faith said, "If it is possible, as far as it depends on you, live at peace with everyone" (Romans 12:18 NIV). That can be a hard thing to do, but that might be exactly why Jesus prayed for our unity. And maybe we should pray that for ourselves as well.

**Discovery**
Our unity with other believers is so the world may know that Jesus is who He said He is.

# RECEIVE
## JOHN 18

**H**ave you ever been somewhere you weren't supposed to be? Maybe you drove down a dead-end road. Maybe you walked into a room and heard a conversation you weren't supposed to hear.

When Jesus was done praying, Judas Iscariot came with soldiers to arrest Him. Jesus gave Himself over and told the soldiers to let His disciples go. The language here implies that the disciples ran away. Jesus was taken to high government officials. Peter followed.

Peter wasn't supposed to be there and yet he was. He was standing outside the high priest's courtyard while Jesus was beginning to be tried. While he stood there, in verse 17, Peter was asked if he was one of Jesus's disciples. He said, "No way!" A little while later, in verse 25, Jesus was asked again if he was Jesus's disciple, and he denied it another time. And a third time, just as

Jesus had predicted, in verse 27, Peter denied Jesus.

Another account of this moment says that Peter and Jesus locked eyes. This disciple wasn't even supposed to be there. He wasn't supposed to be in the position he was. He was supposed to be far away. But he found himself where he shouldn't have been denying the one he said he'd die for. Peter had the chance to share that he knew this Jesus, but because he was in the wrong place, he did something he didn't want to do.

Later in this gospel, John tells of Peter's reconciliation with Jesus. I'm sure that Peter was beating himself up wondering why he would do such a stupid thing like deny Jesus. But in these moments, Peter is an example for each of us to recognize that though we fail even after following Jesus, He offers us forgiveness. Peter was not too far away from receiving forgiveness, and neither are we.

**Discovery**
We are not too far away from receiving forgiveness.

# LIVE
## JOHN 19

Jesus's death was something that no one around Him thought was going to happen, but it has been spoken about for centuries. The disciples could have thought that Jesus was going to overthrow the Roman Empire that was around them and place Himself as King. They were ready for a new political ruler, but they didn't know that Jesus was conquering a bigger authority; the ancient Hebrew text they were familiar with was exactly what had told them about that.

An Old Testament prophet named Zechariah said that the Christ, the Savior, would be betrayed for thirty pieces of silver (Zechariah 11:12–13). John recorded that happening with Judas in John 18.

Another Old Testament prophet by the name of Isaiah would say, "By oppression and judgment he was taken away. Yet who of his generation protested? For he was cut off from the land of the living; for the transgression of my people he was punished" (Isaiah 53:8 NKJV). We read about the trial of Jesus as John recorded it.

A song from the book of Psalms reads that people would gamble for the Savior's clothes. We can read in today's passage: "When the soldiers crucified Jesus, they took his clothes, dividing them into four shares, one for each of them, with the undergarment remaining" (John 19:23 NIV).

The point is that Jesus's death for our sins was something God had planned for way in advance. And that's shown to us in other parts of the Bible for us to understand that Jesus really is who He said He is—the Savior of our lives—and that He came to do what He said He was going to do—to pay for our sin so that we could have new life in Him.

The Bible is a collection of books by a group of Jewish people, but that doesn't make it random. It is a book that points to Jesus. It's about God's redemption for the world through His Son, Jesus Christ. It was the plan from the beginning for Jesus to die to say, "It is finished" (John 19:30 NIV). God's entire goal from the beginning was for Jesus to die so that we may live. The work that God started is fulfilled and completed by Jesus's dying on the cross for us.

### Discovery
God's entire goal from the beginning was for Jesus to die so that we may live.

# PROCLAIM
## JOHN 20

One day after the resurrection, Jesus came to meet with the remaining ten disciples. At that point, Judas has passed away and Thomas just wasn't around. I imagine something important happened like his wanting to catch up on the latest episode of his favorite show.

Jesus came to the other ten disciples. And in this account, Jesus breathed on the disciples giving them the Holy Spirit as He said He would in John 14.

Then Jesus said, "If you forgive anyone's sins, their sins are forgiven; if you do not forgive them, they are not forgiven" (John 20:23 NIV). That was an interesting and strange command. The other gospels—Matthew, Mark, and Luke—say something along the lines of "Go and preach the Gospel" (Matthew 28:19, Mark 16:15, Acts 1:8).

So this seems to mean that the disciples were people who could forgive sins. But in its right context, Jesus didn't say this for the disciples to be the source of forgiveness but rather the stream of it. They weren't commissioned to give forgiveness but to announce it.

Jesus expressed to them and to us that we have an important part in the gospel. We are called by Christ to share the good news of what He did for us. People can't know what God has offered us through Him if we don't proclaim it to them. God has given us the command to tell people that there is forgiveness in Christ, and that's a significant task in which we get to partner with Him!

**Discovery**
People can't know what God has offered us through Him if we don't proclaim it to them.

# MISTAKES
## JOHN 21

**D**o you remember when you were younger and you were scolded for something you shouldn't have done? Maybe you were caught taking a cookie out of the jar right before dinner. Maybe your mom asked you to take the chicken out of the freezer to defrost but the show you were watching was a bit too captivating. Maybe you were supposed to be home before dark and you didn't quite make it.

One of the last times Jesus appeared to His disciples, they all decided to go fishing. When they were cooking their fish on the fire by the sea, Jesus looked over to Peter and asked him, "Do you love me?" (John 21:15 NIV). Peter, always having a deep devotion to Jesus and at that point knowing who He truly was, said that he did love Him. Jesus told him, "Feed my lambs" (John 21:15b NIV). Peter was probably thinking, *I know*

*You're the Good Shepherd and all, but I didn't know You had livestock.*

Jesus asked Peter two more times if he loved Him. Each time, more emphatically, Peter replied that he did. What we can see here is that Jesus asked Peter if he loved Him just as many times as Peter had denied Jesus before His crucifixion. That was done intentionally to show Peter that regardless of what he'd done, Jesus had not given up on him.

Jesus could have spent time wagging His finger at Peter and reminding him that he said that he would never leave Him. But instead, Jesus took the time to show him that regardless of his mistakes, the love of God was greater.

This story is here to show us that our sins and our mistakes are no match for God's love. We are offered an extravagant position to share the love of Christ because of His extravagant love for us.

### Discovery

Our sins and our mistakes are no match for God's love.